Marian Anderson

History Maker Bios

Jane Sutcliffe

⌐ LERNER PUBLICATIONS COMPANY • MINNEAPOLIS

Lerner Publications Company
A division of Lerner Publishing Group, Inc.
241 First Avenue North
Minneapolis, MN 55401 U.S.A.

Website address: www.lernerbooks.com

Library of Congress Cataloging-in-Publication Data

Sutcliffe, Jane.
    Marian Anderson / by Jane Sutcliffe.
       p.   cm. — (History maker biographies)
    Includes bibliographical references (p.) and index.
     ISBN: 978–0–8225–7170–4 (lib. bdg. : alk. paper)
      1. Anderson, Marian, 1897–1993—Juvenile literature. 2. Contraltos—
United States—Biography—Juvenile literature. 3. African American
singers—Biography—Juvenile literature. I. Title.
    ML3930.A5S88 2008
    782.1092—dc22   2007022991

Manufactured in the United States of America
1 2 3 4 5 6 – JR – 13 12 11 10 09 08

TABLE OF CONTENTS

INTRODUCTION

Marian Anderson was a singer. But she was no ordinary singer. She sang for kings and presidents. Her amazing voice thrilled people all over the world.

But some people didn't care about Marian's beautiful voice. All they saw was her black skin. They refused to let her sing in a Washington, D.C., theater. But Marian gave her concert anyway. And this was more than just another concert. On a Sunday afternoon, on the steps of the Lincoln Memorial, Marian Anderson made history.

This is her story.

1 THE GIRL IN THE CHOIR

The little girl closed her eyes. Then she began to sing. Her voice seemed to fill every corner of the Union Baptist Church. The people in the church smiled. They were proud as could be of the girl they called "our Marian."

Marian's parents had this picture taken of Marian in 1898.

Marian Anderson was born on February 27, 1897. She grew up in a friendly neighborhood in Philadelphia, Pennsylvania. Black families and white families lived side by side. Marian and her two little sisters and their friends were in and out of one another's homes all day long.

Every Sunday, Marian joined her father at the Union Baptist Church. (Her mother went to a different church.) When she was six, she joined the children's choir. Singing was just about Marian's favorite thing to do in the world.

Anna Anderson (BACK) poses with her daughters (FROM LEFT TO RIGHT) Ethel, Marian, and Alyse.

Marian didn't sing like the other children though. Her voice seemed as big as the church itself. And she could sing any note. The head of the choir was amazed at Marian's beautiful voice. Before long, she was singing some songs all by herself.

Then, when Marian was twelve, her father died. Her mother worked hard to care for Marian and her sisters.

Money was tight. Marian tried to help. She started singing at neighborhood events. Sometimes she sang at three places in one evening. She received five dollars for each performance. She gave two dollars to her mother and one dollar to each of her sisters. The last dollar she kept for herself.

The more Marian sang, the more people wanted to hear her. By the time she was in high school, she was traveling by train to other cities. She gave concerts at black colleges and churches. Sometimes she was away from home for days.

One evening, after a performance, Marian met a young man named Orpheus Fisher. His nickname was King. Marian and King began spending time together. Soon it was clear that King was in love with Marian. He even suggested that they run off and get married.

Orpheus "King" Fisher studied architecture. He later became a successful architect in New York City.

Marian loved King too. But she was not ready to be a wife. In those days, few women had both a husband and a career. And Marian had already made up her mind. She wanted a career as a singer. Nothing—not even King—was more important.

But if Marian was going to be a concert singer, she needed more than dreams. She needed lessons. She knew that even the best voice could be made better.

Someone told Marian about a music school nearby. To study at a real music school sounded like the most wonderful thing in the world to Marian. She went to the school to see about studying there.

By 1918, many people wanted Marian to perform for their clubs and churches. This picture was taken after she performed a solo in a big concert.

SING HIGH, SING LOW

Singing voices are like bells. Some are clear and high. Others are deep and low. Marian's voice was unusual. She could sing high or low. But she sounded best when she sang the lowest singing parts for girls and women. Those are called the contralto parts.

Marian waited for her turn to apply. But the woman at the desk didn't seem to notice her. She helped all the other students apply. Finally, she looked at Marian.

"What do *you* want?" she snapped. Marian said that she wanted to apply to study at the school.

"We don't take colored," was the woman's sharp reply.

The words stung like a slap. Marian had *never* been treated that way. And just because her skin was a different color! She left without a word.

Marian tried to put music school out of her mind. Then a friend arranged for her to sing for a famous voice teacher. His name was Giuseppe Boghetti. This was a wonderful chance.

It was also a scary one. Mr. Boghetti was rather gruff. He told Marian that he had little time for her. And he certainly had no room in his schedule for another pupil. Then he told her to sing.

Marian did. When she had finished, she could hardly look at Mr. Boghetti. She didn't see his face. But she did hear his words.

"I will make room for you right away," he said.

Giuseppe Boghetti was born in the United States and studied music in Italy. He gave concerts in many European cities before moving back to the United States.

2 MISS 44A

Once a week, Marian saw Mr. Boghetti for her lesson. The lesson was only supposed to be thirty minutes long. But sometimes, if the next student was late, she stayed longer. Marian wanted to learn as much as she could. She wanted every note she sang to be perfect.

Marian's family could not afford books and clothes for school, so she started high school late. She was 24 years old when she graduated with the class of 1921 (ABOVE).

In June 1921, Marian graduated from South Philadelphia High School. She started singing farther and farther from home. Usually she traveled by train. These trips were not always pleasant. Marian often had to travel in the car set aside for African Americans. It was always the worst one on the train. Blacks weren't allowed in hotels either. Marian stayed in private homes.

Mr. Boghetti helped Marian pick out the songs she sang at her concerts. She learned songs in French, Italian, and German. Marian had learned some French in school. Mr. Boghetti helped her with Italian. But she didn't speak a word of German. That made it hard to get the songs right.

Even so, the German songs were her favorite. She loved the sound of the words, even though she didn't know what they meant. Those German songs became Marian's specialty.

Little by little, Marian's name was becoming known. In 1924, Marian decided she was ready to sing in New York. This was an important step. If the New York audience liked her, it would give her career a big boost. Marian practiced for months.

LOUDER, MARIAN!

Marian needed a place all her own where she could practice. She turned an extra bathroom in her house into a music studio. But she was too shy to use it. She was afraid her big voice would bother the neighbors.

Marian was scheduled to sing at the New York Town Hall. On the night of the concert, she walked onto the stage. Then her heart sank. The hall was nearly empty. She could feel her enthusiasm drain from her.

In reviews of the concert, the newspaper critics were not kind. Many noticed that she did not seem to understand the German songs she sang. The critics agreed that she needed to study more.

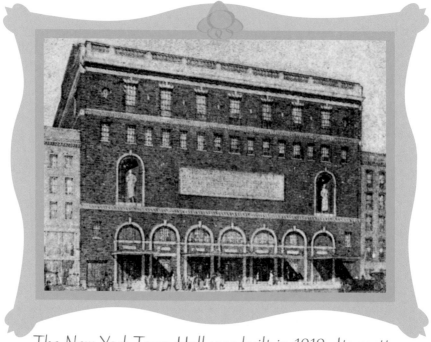

The New York Town Hall was built in 1919. Its motto was "Not a bad seat in the house."

The Town Hall printed a program with Marian's portrait on the cover.

THE TOWN HALL

123 WEST 43rd STREET, NEW YORK, N. Y.

MARIAN ANDERSON
Contralto

Alfred Scott • Publisher • 156 Fifth Avenue, New York

   Marian was shaken. She knew the critics were right. She had not been ready for the concert after all. For months, Marian would not sing. She didn't even want to hear music. Her dream was over.

   She tried to think of something else to do with her life. Of course, there was nothing else. Music meant everything to Marian. It had become a part of her. She could never give it up. And, in time, Marian did begin singing again.

As a soloist, Marian needed fashionable clothing for her concerts. In the early 1920s, women wore loose, flowing dresses and long scarves or strings of beads.

Then Mr. Boghetti entered Marian in a singing contest. Marian was not sure she was ready. But she said yes. She worked harder than ever on the songs she would sing. Three hundred singers were to compete. Marian was number 44A. According to the rules, the judges might listen to only a minute or two of a song. When they were done listening to a singer, they sounded a clicker. Then that person had to stop singing and leave the stage.

Marian's turn came. Her song was called "O mio Fernando." She sang it with half her mind listening for the sound of the clicker. It never came. She was allowed to finish. Then a voice floated down from the balcony. "Does 44A have another song?" Marian sang again.

A few days, later the news came. She was one of sixteen semifinalists. Once more, she sang for the judges.

This time, four finalists were to be chosen. Together, Marian and Mr. Boghetti waited for some news. Then the phone rang. When Mr. Boghetti hung up, he ran to Marian. "We have won!" he shouted. "There will be no finals."

On August 26, 1925, Marian got her prize. She appeared in a grand concert in New York. Her whole family was there to see her. Even King Fisher came.

Marian sang with ease. When she finished "O mio Fernando," the musicians tapped on their music stands. It was their way of honoring her. The sound meant more to Marian than the thunder of applause.

3 MARIAN FEVER

Marian had had one big success. She was ready for more. At first, that's just what happened. She was invited to sing as far away as the West Coast.

But after a while, the invitations stopped. Soon she was singing at the same churches and colleges as before. Marian felt her career was standing still.

Worst of all, she was having the same problem with her German songs. Critics kept saying that she didn't seem to understand what she was singing.

Marian had to do something. She decided to take a very big step. In October 1927, Marian sailed for Great Britain. She planned to study with a well-known teacher of German songs.

But almost as soon as she started her lessons, the teacher fell sick. That was the end of the lessons. After that, Marian spent her time singing for small groups of friends she'd made. In September 1928, she went home again. She didn't have much to show for her trip.

During her first visit to Britain, Marian toured with John Payne (RIGHT), another singer from the United States.

There was only one thing to do. In June 1930, Marian went back to Europe. This time, she went to Germany. She stayed with a couple who spoke little English. Soon Marian was learning all kinds of German words.

She found a teacher and studied German songs too. Little by little, the songs began to make sense to Marian. One day, she was with her teacher when two men came to listen. They were looking for talented young singers to perform in concerts. And they liked what they heard.

Marian studied with Kurt Johnen (RIGHT), an expert in German music. He taught her how to sing in German.

Helmer Enwall (MIDDLE) was one of the men who arranged Marian's Scandinavian tour. He and his wife, Therese (RIGHT), traveled around Europe with Marian. They remained her friends for many years.

The men asked Marian to sing in a part of northern Europe called Scandinavia. She was to give six concerts throughout Norway, Sweden, Finland, and Denmark. No black singer had ever performed there. Marian would be the first.

From the minute Marian stepped onto the stage in Norway, she was a sensation. The audience loved her. The applause went on and on. People cheered for more. After the concert, many people sent flowers and gifts to her hotel room.

During her tour of Scandinavia, Marian visited a farm in Finland.

Marian's concerts quickly sold out. Just as quickly, more were added. Instead of six concerts, she gave more than a dozen in three weeks.

All too soon, it was over. Marian had to go home. Her career in the United States hadn't changed a bit. No one seemed to care about her success in Scandinavia. She was singing at the same churches and colleges as always.

But people in Scandinavia were begging her to return. Once more, Marian knew what she had to do. In 1933, she went back to Scandinavia to sing.

Last time, Marian had been a sensation. This time, she was a star. People stood in line all night for a chance to buy tickets to her concerts. Police had to hold back the crowds wherever she appeared. Even the king of Sweden came to see what all the fuss was about. Newspapers were calling it "Marian Fever."

Kosti Vehanen (LEFT) played the piano for all Marian's Scandinavian tour performances. He was from Finland.

For the next seven months, Marian sang. She gave more than one hundred concerts—sometimes as many as five concerts in five days. But she wasn't tired at all. She was excited. *This* was the career she had dreamed of.

After Scandinavia, Marian toured other parts of Europe. In each country, her concerts were a success. In Austria, the famous conductor Arturo Toscanini was in the audience. He told her, "A voice like yours is heard once in a hundred years."

In 1935, near the end of her tour of Europe, Marian performed in Budapest, Hungary.

Marian always ended her concerts with songs called spirituals. These were songs that were once sung by African American slaves. Marian sang these songs with great feeling. Sometimes her audience was left in tears.

By December 1935, Marian was ready to go home. She had been in Europe for two years. Marian had been a success there. She would also try to find success in her own country. And her first concert would be in a very familiar place—the New York Town Hall.

4 EASTER SUNDAY 1939

Eleven years had passed since Marian had last stepped onto the stage of the New York Town Hall. The concert there had been a disaster for her. On December 30, 1935, she stood on the stage of that same hall again.

This time, things were different. Every seat in the hall was filled. And the audience loved her. Their cheers told Marian what she needed to hear. This concert was a success.

Critics agreed. One called her "one of the great singers of our time." He reminded people that Europe had praised Marian. "It is time for her own country to honor her," he said.

SINGING WITH A SECRET

At her Town Hall concert, Marian had a secret. She had slipped and fallen on the ship from Europe. Her ankle was broken. Her beautiful long dress hid the cast on her leg. But Marian refused to let anyone tell the audience. She didn't want anyone to think she was asking people to feel sorry for her. She wanted to be judged for her singing alone.

In 1938, Marian received an honorary degree in music from Howard University in Washington, D.C.

Suddenly, Marian was in demand. She gave concerts in cities all over the country. In her home city of Philadelphia, a crowd of reporters and photographers mobbed her dressing room. She even sang at the White House for President Franklin Roosevelt and the First Lady.

In 1939, Marian planned a concert in Washington, D.C. She had many fans there. She needed a very big hall to hold them all. Marian's concert manager went to the largest hall in the city, Constitution Hall. It was owned by a patriotic group called the Daughters of the American Revolution (DAR).

Marian's manager received a shocking reply. The DAR would let only white singers use the hall. Marian was not allowed to sing there. The story was front-page news around the country. People wrote angry letters to newspapers about the DAR.

The First Lady, Eleanor Roosevelt, was a member of the DAR. She knew the group's decision was wrong. She wanted to take a stand. She left the DAR. And she announced her decision in the newspapers.

Still, the DAR would not back down. Reporters pestered Marian with questions. They expected her to say bitter things about the DAR. But Marian wouldn't. She didn't feel bitter. She simply felt sad.

Eleanor Roosevelt was a leading member of the DAR. She spoke at its convention in 1934.

Then government officials stepped in. They invited Marian to give a free outdoor concert. She could sing on the steps of the Lincoln Memorial. The memorial was the perfect place to send a message about justice and freedom. Marian agreed to do the concert there.

The concert was scheduled for Easter Sunday, April 9. That morning, Marian arrived in Washington. She got ready for the concert at a private home. No hotel in the city would take her.

The DAR had Constitution Hall built in 1928. The first performance there took place in 1929.

A huge crowd gathered at the Lincoln Memorial to hear Marian's concert.

When she arrived at the Lincoln Memorial, police made a path for her through the crowd. She went to a little room in the memorial. She looked over her songs. Then it was time to go before the crowd.

There were people as far as she could see. The crowd stretched from the steps of the Lincoln Memorial all the way to the Washington Monument. That was a quarter of a mile away. And they were all standing on tiptoe and craning their necks for a glimpse of her.

Radio stations broadcasted Marian's concert at the Lincoln Memorial to millions of listeners.

For one horrible moment, Marian couldn't remember the words to her first song. Then the music started. She closed her eyes. Then Marian sang.

My country, 'tis of thee,
Sweet land of liberty . . .

She stood straight and proud as she sang. Microphones carried her rich, beautiful voice to the crowd. Every word was crisp and clear. She sang other songs too. One was her old favorite, "O mio Fernando."

Then the concert came to an end. The cheers of the crowd went on and on. Marian hadn't planned to say anything. But she was so moved, she told the crowd, "I can't tell you what you have done for me today. I thank you from the bottom of my heart again and again."

Seventy-five thousand people came to hear Marian sing that day. Millions more heard her on the radio. That concert made Marian a bigger star than she had ever dreamed of becoming. For the rest of her life, people would come up to her and say, "You know, I was at that Easter concert."

The audience stretched as far as Marian could see.

5 WHAT SHE HAD WAS SINGING

Marian's concert gave people hope. She showed people that they could stand up for what was right with pride and dignity. Three months after her Easter concert, she won a special award. The Spingarn Medal was given each year to a black American for a great accomplishment. Eleanor Roosevelt presented her with the medal.

Marian and King lived at Marianna Farm in Danbury, Connecticut, after their wedding.

Marian was busier than ever. People all over the world wanted to hear the famous Marian Anderson. But she did make time for one special person.

King Fisher had been in love with Marian for more than twenty years. He still wanted to marry her. At last, Marian was ready. In July 1943, they were married. They both enjoyed their life at Marianna Farm, the big farm they had bought in Connecticut.

Marian didn't get to spend much time there, though. Concerts kept her away from home. She had many fans, both black and white.

MARIAN'S GIFT

Over the years, Marian received many honors. One gave her special pride. In 1941, she received the Philadelphia Award from her home city. The award is given to an outstanding Philadelphia citizen. And it came with a $10,000 prize. Marian used the money to start a fund for young singers. She was happy that her prize would help talented young people for years to come.

In some places, especially in the South, that was a problem. Some cities did not allow black and white people to sit together. Often black listeners sat on one side of the hall. White listeners sat on the other. It was as if an invisible line had been drawn right down the middle.

Marian was never happy singing in places like that. Finally she decided she had had enough. She made a new rule. People would sit together—or she wouldn't sing.

And she stuck to it. When she sang in Florida in 1952, black and white fans sat together. It was the first time that had ever been allowed in that state.

By then, Marian was known as the world's greatest contralto. Many of the songs she sang were from famous operas. Marian loved these thrilling plays told with songs instead of spoken words. But she had never sung as a member of the cast in an opera.

Marian had many beautiful costumes made for her concerts. In this picture, she waits for a tailor to finish fitting her dress.

Then one night, Marian went to a party. The head of the famous New York Metropolitan Opera was there too. His name was Rudolf Bing. He went right up to Marian.

"Would you be interested in singing with the Metropolitan?" he asked her.

Marian was surprised. No black singer had ever appeared with the Met.

"I think I would," she said.

With that, things happened fast. Marian would play the part of a magician, or sorceress. She not only had to learn the songs she would sing. She also had to learn to act the part. Marian had never been so busy in her life.

Rudolf Bing (RIGHT) was the general manager of the Metropolitan Opera. Marian began rehearsing there in 1954.

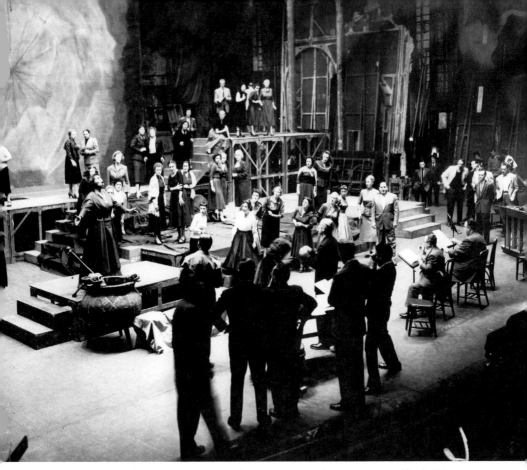

Marian (SINGING, AT LEFT) practices the opera called UN BALLO IN MASCHERA, which is Italian for "A MASKED BALL."

On January 7, 1955, Marian had her big night. She was almost never nervous before her concerts. But this time she was.

The audience didn't seem to notice. When she appeared, they applauded for five minutes. Marian couldn't start her song until all the cheering had ended.

Marian gave her final concert at Carnegie Hall. She sang a beautiful song called "Ave Maria."

Marian was proud of her chance to sing in the opera. She called it a highlight of her life. She had been singing nearly all of that life. Marian was getting tired. In 1965, when she was sixty-eight, she gave her last concert. Then she went home to King and the farm.

But people did not forget her. For the rest of her life, Marian received honors and awards. In 1991, she received a special Grammy Award, given to her by other singers and musicians. The award recognized her life spent making music.

On April 8, 1993, Marian died at the age of ninety-six. She died one day before the fifty-fourth anniversary of her famous Easter concert.

Marian's concert would always be remembered as an important step in the fight for equal rights for all Americans. But Marian never thought of herself as a fighter. "What I had was singing," she said—not fighting. But she had fought battles. She forced open doors that had been closed to African Americans. She did it with her amazing voice. She did it with her quiet dignity. Marian led the way through those doors for others to follow.

Marian (CENTER) met many U.S. presidents. In 1992, she met with President George H.W. Bush and Barbara Bush.

TIMELINE

MARIAN ANDERSON WAS
BORN ON FEBRUARY 27,
1897.

In the year . . .

1903   Marian joined the Junior Choir at the Union Baptist Church.

1910   her father died.

1921   she began singing lessons with Giuseppe Boghetti.

1924   she first appeared at the New York Town Hall.

1925   she won a singing competition in New York. | Age 28 |

1930   she went to Germany to study German songs.

she toured Scandinavia for the first time.

1933   she toured Scandinavia and parts of Europe.

1935   she sang at the New York Town Hall a second time.

1936   she sang at the White House for President Franklin Roosevelt and his wife, Eleanor.

1939   she gave a free concert on the steps on the Lincoln Memorial on Easter Sunday. | Age 42 |

1943   she married King Fisher.

1955   she became the first black singer to sing a part with the Metropolitan Opera. | Age 58 |

1965   she gave her last concert in New York.

1993   she died on April 8, 1993. | Age 96 |

NOW APPEARING
AT CONSTITUTION HALL . . .

In 1952, Constitution Hall dropped its "white singers only" rule. Marian sang there many times after that. But she never felt that she had won a victory. She simply felt that she had the right to be there as a talented singer.

Marian's nephew followed her into a career in music. He performed at Constitution Hall too. Once he called his Aunt Marian from there. He knew how she had struggled to sing at the hall. He told her how easy it had been for him. All he had to do was park his car and walk in.

"Well, dear heart," Marian said, "I'm just delighted that some things have changed."

And they have, in part, because of Marian Anderson.

Marian's nephew, James De Priest, conducts an orchestra.

FURTHER READING

Ferris, Jeri. *What I Had Was Singing: The Story of Marian Anderson.* Minneapolis: Carolrhoda Books, 1994. This biography tells the story of Marian's rise to fame.

McKissack, Pat, and Fredrick McKissack. *Marian Anderson: A Great Singer.* Berkeley Heights, NJ: Enslow Publishers, 2001. This short biography includes many illustrations and pictures from Marian's life.

Muñoz Ryan, Pam. *When Marian Sang: The True Recital of Marian Anderson.* New York: Scholastic Press, 2002. This picture book uses lyrics from Marian's songs to tell her life story.

WEBSITES

Marian Anderson Historical Society
http://www.mariananderson.org
Listen to recordings of Marian's performances at the official website of the Marian Anderson Historical Society.

Marian Anderson: A Life in Song
http://www.library.upenn.edu/exhibits/rbm/anderson/
View an online exhibit with pictures from Marian's photo albums.

SELECT BIBLIOGRAPHY

Anderson, Marian. *My Lord, What a Morning: An Autobiography.* Chicago: University of Illinois Press, 1956.

Ardley, Neil. *Music: An Illustrated Encyclopedia.* New York: Facts on File, 1986.

Chenu, Bruno. *The Trouble I've Seen: The Big Book of Negro Spirituals.* Valley Forge, PA: Judson Press, 2003.

Coleman, Emily. "Marian Anderson: A Voice Became a Symbol." *Newsweek,* April 25, 1949, 84–86.

Freedman, Russell. *The Voice That Challenged a Nation: Marian Anderson and the Struggle for Equal Rights.* New York: Clarion Books, 2004.

Keiler, Allan. *Marian Anderson: A Singer's Journey.* New York: Scribner, 2000.

Klaw, Barbara. "A Voice One Hears Once in a Hundred Years: An Interview with Marian Anderson." *American Heritage,* February 1977, 50–57.

Taubman, Howard. "Marian Anderson in Concert Here." *New York Times,* Dec. 31, 1935, 13.

Time. "In Egypt Land." Dec. 30, 1946, 59–61.

Vehanen, Kosti. *Marian Anderson: A Portrait.* Westport, CT: Greenwood Press, Publishers, 1941.

INDEX

Acknowledgments

For photographs and artwork: © Metronome/Hulton Archive/Getty Images, p. 4; Marian Anderson Collection/Rare Book & Manuscript Library/University of Pennsylvania, pp. 7, 8, 9, 10, 12, 14, 17, 18, 21, 22, 23, 24, 25, 26, 30, 37, 40, 41, 43, 45; Rare Book & Manuscript Library/University of Pennsylvania, p.16; AP Photo, p. 31; © Thomas D. Mcavoy/Time Life Pictures/Getty Images, pp. 32, 33; © Everett Collection, p. 34; © Bettmann/CORBIS, p. 35; © Lofman/Pix Inc./Time Life Pictures/Getty Images, p. 39; AP Photo/Dave Pickoff, p. 42.

Front cover: © Bettmann/CORBIS
Back cover: Marian Anderson Collection/Rare Book & Manuscript Library/University of Pennsylvania

For quoted material: pp. 6, 11, 12, 19 (both quotes), 35 (both quotes), 40 (both quotes), 45, *Marian Anderson, My Lord, What a Morning: An Autobiography* (Chicago: University of Illinois Press, 1956); p. 29, Howard Taubman, "Marian Anderson in Concert Here," *The New York Times,* Dec. 31, 1935; p. 43, Barbara Klaw, "A Voice One Hears Once in a Hundred Years: An Interview with Marian Anderson," *American Heritage,* February 1977.